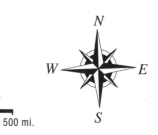

W9-AVI-392

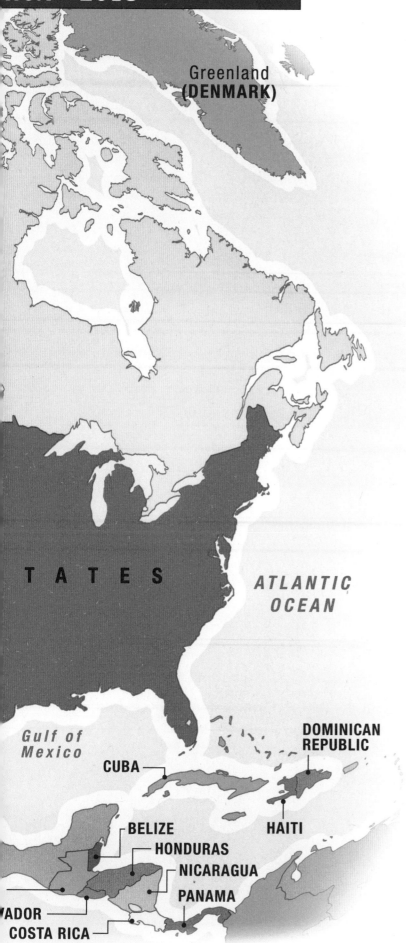

Greenland
(DENMARK)

T A T E S

*ATLANTIC
OCEAN*

*Gulf of
Mexico*

CUBA

**DOMINICAN
REPUBLIC**

BELIZE

HAITI

HONDURAS

NICARAGUA

PANAMA

ADOR

COSTA RICA

The name *America*
comes from the Italian
explorer Amerigo
Vespucci. Amerigo
Vespucci was one
of the first explorers
to sail across the
Atlantic Ocean and
visit what is now
called North America.

0   500 km.

0   500 mi.

N

W   *E*

S

4

BODIES OF WATER IN NORTH AMERICA

Think about a body of water you know. (A body of water in nature, that is. Swimming pools don't count!) What do you know about it? Is it big or small? Can you see land on the other side? Does the water flow, or is it still? Is that water salty or fresh? The answers to these and other questions can help you figure out what kind of body of water it is.

Check out the bodies of water on this map. Which body of water do you live closest to?

ARCTIC OCEAN

PACIFIC OCEAN

Rio Grande

PACIFIC OCEAN

Atlantic and Pacific Oceans

The largest bodies of water are oceans. Oceans cover much of Earth's surface. You can't drink the water in an ocean. Why? Oceans contain salt water.

North America borders on three oceans. The Arctic Ocean is to the north. The Pacific Ocean is the largest ocean. The Atlantic Ocean is the second-largest ocean.

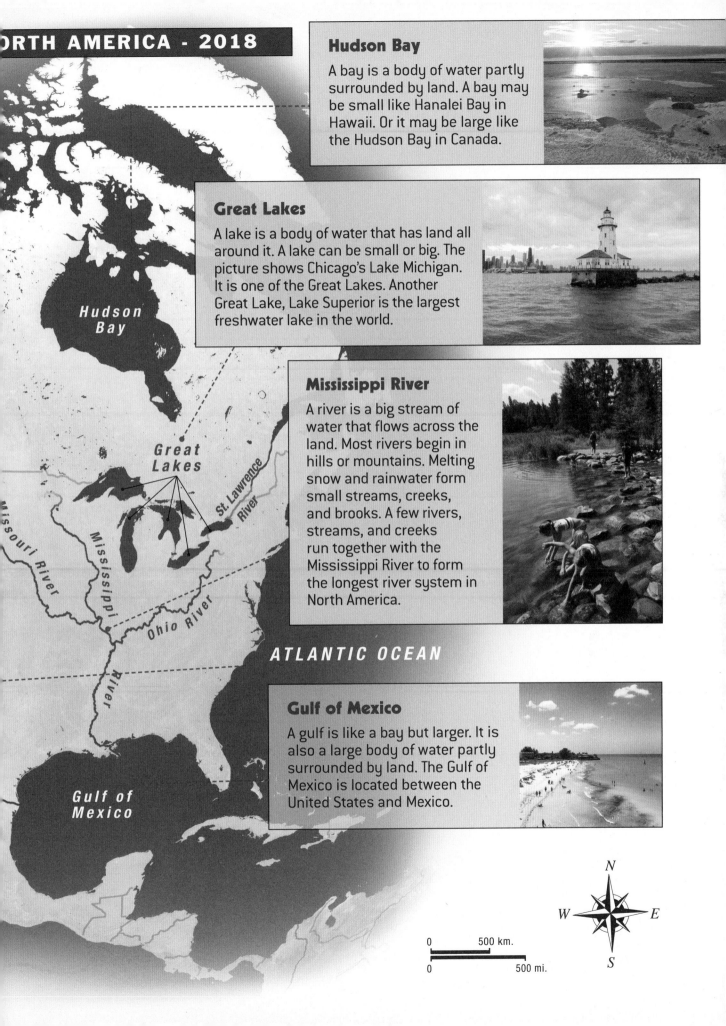

Hudson Bay

A bay is a body of water partly surrounded by land. A bay may be small like Hanalei Bay in Hawaii. Or it may be large like the Hudson Bay in Canada.

Great Lakes

A lake is a body of water that has land all around it. A lake can be small or big. The picture shows Chicago's Lake Michigan. It is one of the Great Lakes. Another Great Lake, Lake Superior is the largest freshwater lake in the world.

Mississippi River

A river is a big stream of water that flows across the land. Most rivers begin in hills or mountains. Melting snow and rainwater form small streams, creeks, and brooks. A few rivers, streams, and creeks run together with the Mississippi River to form the longest river system in North America.

ATLANTIC OCEAN

Gulf of Mexico

A gulf is like a bay but larger. It is also a large body of water partly surrounded by land. The Gulf of Mexico is located between the United States and Mexico.

Hudson Bay

Great Lakes

St. Lawrence River

Missouri River

Mississippi River

Ohio River

Gulf of Mexico

N
W   E
S

0   500 km.

0   500 mi.

LANDFORMS IN NORTH AMERICA

How would you describe the land where you live? Are you in the mountains or in a valley? Maybe you live on the plains or near rolling hills. Mountains, valleys, hills, and plains are examples of landforms. A landform is a kind of land with a special shape. Suppose you could take a trip across North America in a plane. What landforms would you see?

Denali

Denali is the tallest mountain in North America. It is snow-covered all year long.

Rocky Mountains

A hill is land that rises up above the land around it. A mountain is a very high hill. The Rockies are a mountain range, or group of mountains, that stretch across Canada and the United States. As you might guess from its name, the Rocky Mountains are tall and rocky. Many of its mountaintops are covered in snow all year.

Great Plains

A plain is a large area of flat land. The Great Plains includes parts of 10 states and parts of Canada. This land is good for growing crops such as corn and wheat.

Appalachian Mountains

The Appalachians are older than the Rocky Mountains. Over time, their sharp peaks have worn down.

Shenandoah Valley

A valley is low land between mountains. Many valleys are green with plants and trees.

USING A LANDFORM MAP

Maps are great for finding the location of places. But did you know that maps can also give information about a place? Take a look at this landform map of North America. How do the different parts of the map help you?

A map title tells you what the map shows.

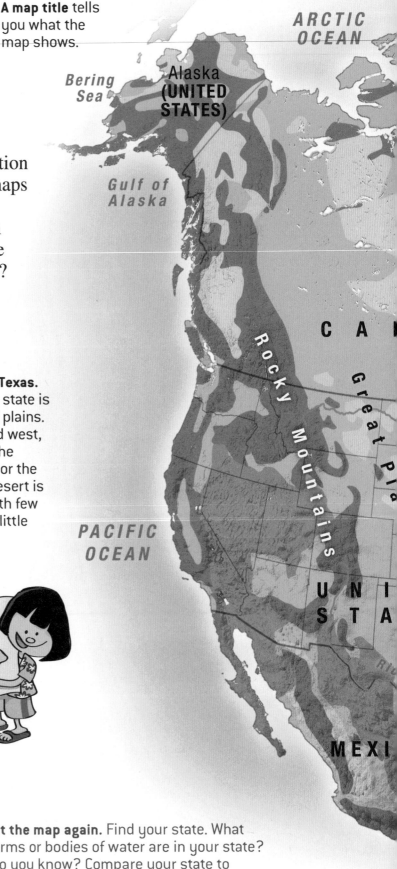

ARCTIC OCEAN

Bering Sea

Alaska **(UNITED STATES)**

Gulf of Alaska

C A

Rocky Mountains

Great Pla

PACIFIC OCEAN

U N I
S T A

MEXI

← **I live in Texas.** Most of my state is made up of plains. But if I head west, I can visit the mountains or the desert. A desert is dry land with few plants and little rainfall.

↓ **I live in Hawaii.** Hawaii is a state made up of several islands. An island is a landform that is completely surrounded by water. Greenland is also an island. In fact, it is the largest island in the world that is not a continent!

Hawaii **(UNITED STATES)**

Look at the map again. Find your state. What landforms or bodies of water are in your state? How do you know? Compare your state to other regions of North America. A region is an area of land that has the same features.

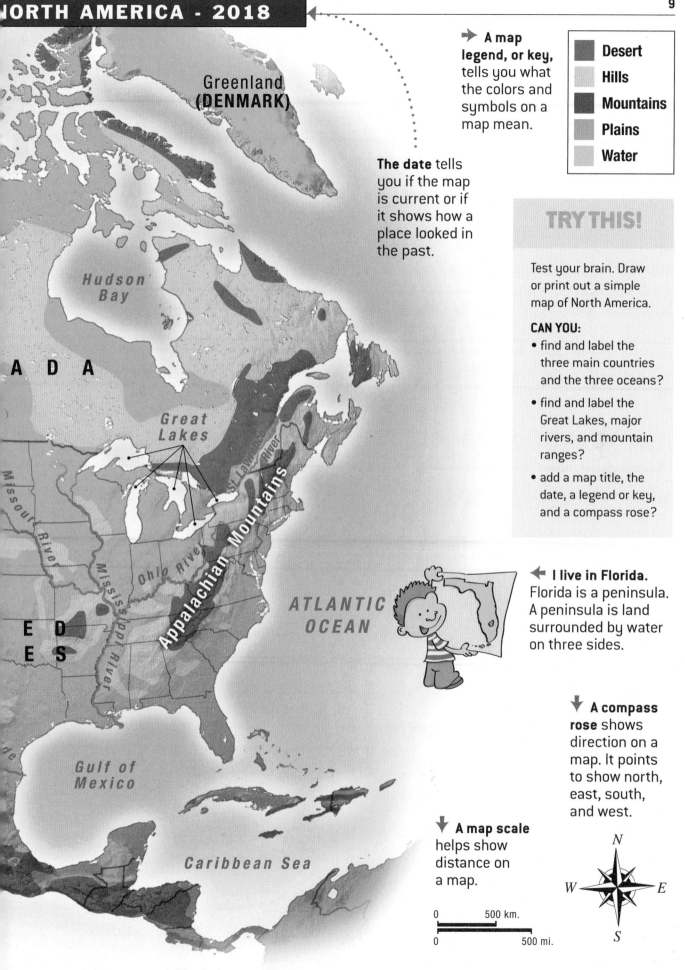

A map legend, or key, tells you what the colors and symbols on a map mean.

	Desert
	Hills
	Mountains
	Plains
	Water

The date tells you if the map is current or if it shows how a place looked in the past.

TRY THIS!

Test your brain. Draw or print out a simple map of North America.

CAN YOU:
- find and label the three main countries and the three oceans?
- find and label the Great Lakes, major rivers, and mountain ranges?
- add a map title, the date, a legend or key, and a compass rose?

I live in Florida. Florida is a peninsula. A peninsula is land surrounded by water on three sides.

A compass rose shows direction on a map. It points to show north, east, south, and west.

A map scale helps show distance on a map.

Map labels: Greenland (DENMARK), Hudson Bay, CANADA, Great Lakes, St. Lawrence River, Missouri River, Mississippi River, Ohio River, Appalachian Mountains, UNITED STATES, ATLANTIC OCEAN, Gulf of Mexico, Caribbean Sea

0   500 km.
0   500 mi.

N W E S

NORTH AMERICA FROM SPACE

Maps are a great way to see all of North America at one time. But if you were an astronaut, you could take a picture of North America that is out of this world!

SEASONS AND CLIMATE

What is it like outside right now? Will the weather be the same when the seasons change? The answers depend on where you live.

Weather is what the air is like outside. Two things cause weather: the sun and moisture. Together, they make clouds form. Clouds can bring rain, snow, sleet, or hail. During the day, the sun may be behind the clouds. When clouds move, the sun shines.

What is your weather like from year to year? Do you have warm, sunny days nearly all the time? Or are your winters freezing? These questions are all about climate and seasons.

Climate is the pattern of weather in an area over a long period. Different places have different climates. The climate of a place depends on how much rain it gets and how warm it is during a year.

A season is a time of year that has a certain kind of weather. In many places, the weather changes with each season. The four seasons are spring, summer, fall, and winter.

The colors on this map show different climate areas. Find where you live on the map. What kind of climate do you have?

ARCTIC OCEAN

Alaska (UNITED STATES)

Gulf of Alaska

PACIFIC OCEAN

C A

U N
S T

MEXIC

Legend:
- Polar
- Continental
- Dry
- Mild
- Tropical

Tropical

Places with tropical climates are very warm all year round. They are close to the equator. In tropical climates, winter is not too different from summer. It's always hot!

Hawaii (UNITED STATES)

Greenland
(DENMARK)

Hudson
Bay

A D A

T E D
T E S

ATLANTIC
OCEAN

Gulf of
Mexico

CUBA

Caribbean Sea

Polar

Places with a polar climate are, you guessed it, near the North or South Pole. Summers may be cool in some places, but other polar areas are freezing all year round.

Continental

Places far from an ocean often have a continental climate. They get long, freezing winters and short, hot summers.

Mild

Much of the United States has a mild climate. Some mild places are hot in summer and cool in winter. Others have warm summers and cold winters. Places in the U.S. with colder winters are mostly farther north.

Dry

Dry places get little rain. The hottest places in the world have dry climates. But some dry places can be quite cold.

0   500 km.

0   500 mi.

N
W   E
S

WHAT GROWS THERE?

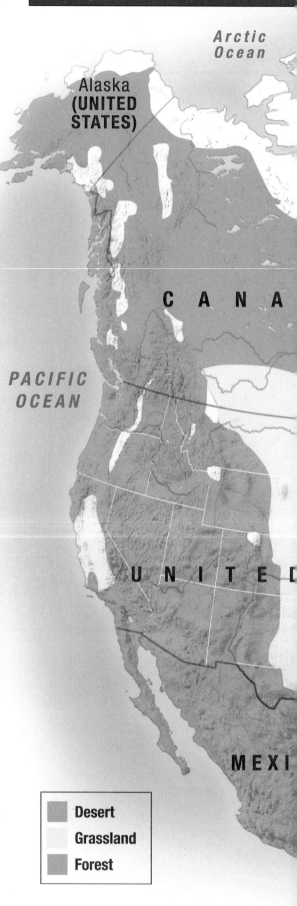

What does the country near your home look like? Do you see lots of trees? Or are there mostly grassy fields? Or is the land rocky with just a cactus or two?

Plants grow in the region where they get the rain and warmth they need to grow. Different regions have different kinds of plants. Three main plant regions in North America are forests, grasslands, and deserts.

What plant region do you live in? Take a look at this map. It shows where to find each plant region in North America.

- Desert
- Grassland
- Forest

Most places that get less than 15 inches of rain a year are deserts. Some deserts are hot. Farther north, deserts are cool.

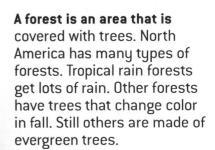

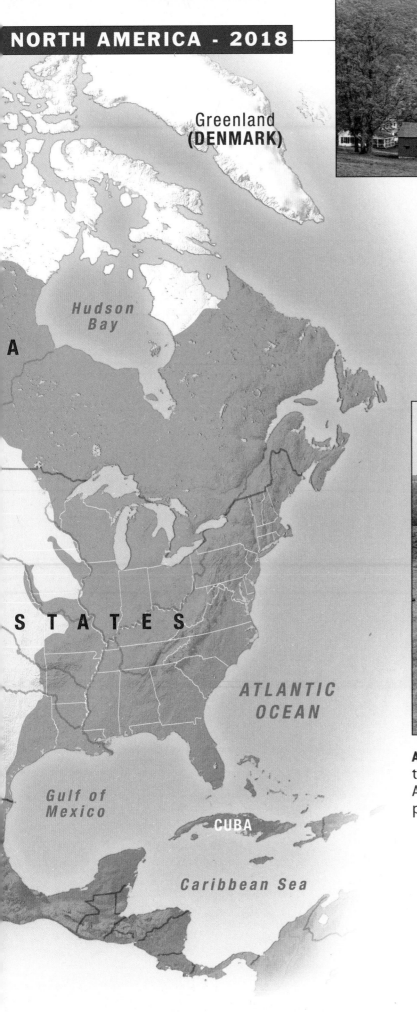

Greenland
(DENMARK)

Hudson
Bay

A

S T A T E S

ATLANTIC
OCEAN

Gulf of
Mexico

CUBA

Caribbean Sea

A forest is an area that is covered with trees. North America has many types of forests. Tropical rain forests get lots of rain. Other forests have trees that change color in fall. Still others are made of evergreen trees.

A grassland is, you guessed it, an area, that is covered with grass. In North America, grasslands are also called prairies or plains.

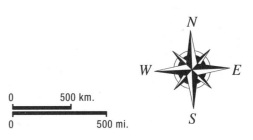

N
W   E
S

0   500 km.

0   500 mi.

WORLD REGIONS

Now that you've explored North America, are you ready to go bigger? How do regions in North America compare to other regions in the world? To begin, look at a globe. A globe is a model of Earth. Like a map, it shows areas of land and water. It also shows the location of the North and South Poles and the equator. The equator is an imaginary line that divides Earth into northern and southern halves.

➤ **Trying to see the whole** world at once on a globe is enough to make your head (and the globe) spin. Instead, the maps here can help. Regions near the equator are hot all year round. Regions close to the North and South Poles are cold all year round.

Each region of the world has its own landforms and climate. Let's take a look at some of the biggest, longest, and coldest places in the world.

The Grand Canyon is one of the longest and deepest canyons in the world.

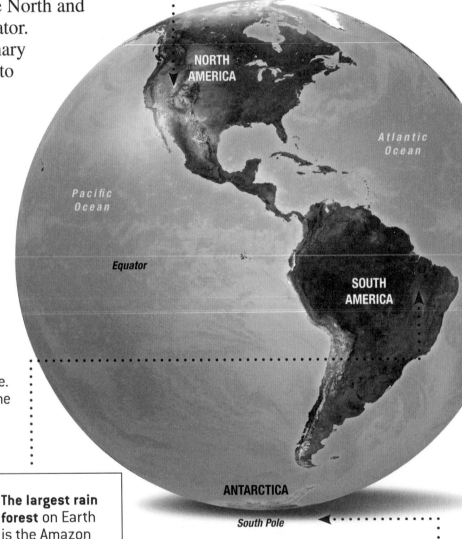

North Pole

NORTH AMERICA

Atlantic Ocean

Pacific Ocean

Equator

SOUTH AMERICA

ANTARCTICA

South Pole

The largest rain forest on Earth is the Amazon rain forest. It covers much of northern South America. In some places, as much as 400 inches of rain fall in a year. That's over 30 feet of rain!

At the South Pole, Antarctica is the coldest continent. Ice covers almost all of it. Winter temperatures average −74°F. A research station on Antarctica recorded the coldest temperature ever, −128°F. Now that's cold!

The Sahara is the largest desert in the world. It covers most of northern Africa. Some of this land gets only a half an inch of rain a year.

Mount Everest is in the Himalayas, a mountain range in Asia. It is the highest mountain on Earth — 29,035 feet above sea level. That's higher than some planes can fly!

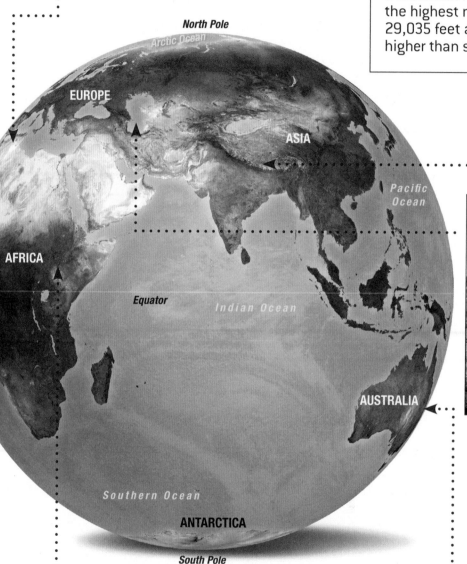

The Caspian Sea is the largest lake in the world. Unlike most lakes, it contains salt water.

The Nile River is the world's longest river. It flows north through parts of 10 countries and empties into the Mediterranean Sea.

Australia is the only continent that is also made up of one country. It is the flattest and driest continent. Deserts cover most of the continent. You may know it for its unique animals, such as the kangaroo.

Activities

MAKE A MAP

How can someone discover interesting places found in North America? With a map, of course! A map is a great way to learn more about parts of our world. Your job is to draw your own map of North America. Use symbols and colors to mark locations of some landforms, mountain ranges, Great Lakes, and major rivers that you want to show. Label the countries and oceans. Make sure to date your map and give it a title. Include a legend, a scale, and a compass rose.

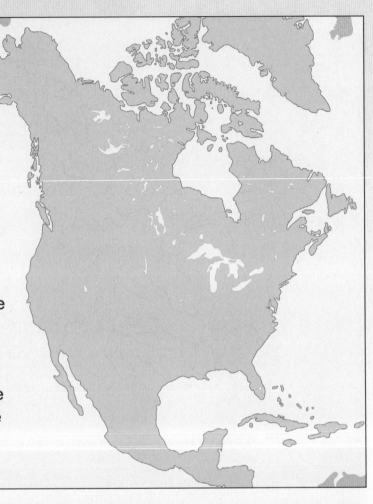

WEATHER REPORTER

As the seasons change, what is the weather like where you live? How can you tell when it is spring, summer, fall, and winter? Do you notice differences in the temperature outside? Be a weather reporter to share what you feel and see. Choose two different seasons to write about. In sentences, describe how the two seasons are alike and how they are different. Then share your weather report with your classmates.